The World Is Mostly Sky

The World Is Mostly Sky

Sarah Ens

TURNSTONE PRESS

The World Is Mostly Sky
copyright © Sarah Ens 2020
Turnstone Press
Artspace Building
206-100 Arthur Street
Winnipeg, MB
R3B 1H3 Canada
www.TurnstonePress.com

Turnstone Press gratefully acknowledges the assistance of the Canada Council for the Arts, the Manitoba Arts Council, the Government of Canada through the Canada Book Fund, and the Province of Manitoba through the Book Publishing Tax Credit and the Book Publisher Marketing Assistance Program.

The epigraph on page 52 is from "The Glass Essay" by Anne Carson, from GLASS, IRONY, AND GOD, copyright ©1995 by Anne Carson. Reprinted by permission of New Directions Publishing Corp.

Cover design: Melissa McIvor

Printed and bound in Canada.

Library and Archives Canada Cataloguing in Publication

Title: The world is mostly sky / Sarah Ens.
Names: Ens, Sarah, 1992- author.
Description: Poems.
Identifiers: Canadiana (print) 20190233184 | Canadiana (ebook) 20190233192 | ISBN 9780888017055 (softcover) | ISBN 9780888017062 (EPUB) | ISBN 9780888017079 (Kindle) | ISBN 9780888017086 (PDF)
Classification: LCC PS8609.N72 W67 2020 | DDC C811/.6—dc23

MANITOBA ARTS COUNCIL
CONSEIL DES ARTS DU MANITOBA

Canada Council for the Arts Conseil des arts du Canada

Funded by the Government of Canada
Financé par le gouvernement du Canada
Canada

Manitoba

for my sisters

a boat is not

the whole world

(the world

is mostly

sky)

Contents

Silos

Wuthering: A Comprehensive Guide

Powerful Millennials on the California Freeway

The World Is Mostly Sky

By the Skin

I have pulled out my own teeth
    called them tenderly as disciples   each
    the hollow hurt of bone

I have given them to certain friends & family
    in square white envelopes *here*   *have these things*
    I grew in my sleep here   *take all the yanking in me*

& I've buried one behind each apartment I've lived in
    hoping they'll grow into the skeletons of words
    but bend like breath in the breeze

I suppose I am wishing for each stone of me
    to become something sound   *aha* I say
    with my mouth too wide *here*   *see my biting gifts*
    these baby promise pearls   *these hard little dreams*

Silos

Always Trees with the Almighty

In the woods behind our house
was a tree that looked like God

pressed a cigarette clean through
its trunk. Struck by lightning,

we were told, but Act of God
is what we knew, squeezed

into the maple's split centre,
mouth, meaning portal,

password, peek.
Each Eden

rooted out of reach,
we tore mittens thundering

up icy bark, snapped branches
& bones, named everything

we could scale, see,
so easily set ablaze.

World We Rise

i.

we practice our poplar
branch   swinging
in sequence
                                in &
                out
                                roll   duck
                                & squat
                broad stories
between us:
the neighbour
               kid
               my sister &
               me   racing
helicopter seeds
from   the treehouse

waving to
robin   returned
               her fluffy
                                 sing-
                                 song
breast brooding us

               under   the watch of the world

                                 we rise

ii.

lie in the wet   grass
by the woods
            & wait
            for each year's
hidden hatching

                    startle
when some teen
            steps too close
scoping   sizing
his stick's sharp
            reach
            & then

                         death

sweeps   once   twice
            the nest
            warm with
down

we

just

fold

over

iii.

scream
into sweaters
silence
at the splatter

fingers pulling blue
shell

from milky yolk
mother
frantic
at the hydro
wire
feet
clicking
clenching spring
sky
with shrieks

hot
blood
round &
round
in her

iv.

did she

think she

could still

save them

          & us

Floriculture

My mother
(spent summers kneeling)
took pride in my muddy crunching,
(between carrots/potatoes/beans/
radishes/raspberries/peas) my reaching
to the earth. I do love
the pulling up, (& sometimes
I'd help pluck, wary of worms)
but the truth is I am not good
at the waiting, watching,
(that tongue-pink poking)
hard work of hope,
so I want to learn, at least,
(armed with salt) the shapes
of the sounds, tend the promise,
always, of words—

(to wither every last threat.
My mother would show me)
hydrangea/begonia/carnation/peony/
(how slugs & bugs chewed
through seedlings, how)
snapdragon/geranium/
(poplars stretched shadows,
how rabbits stole) tiger lily/lilac/
lotus/chrysanthemum—
(her most tender) names that
(labour & bloom)
knuckle roots over rocks,
(& then she'd try to show me)

names
(*here*, pointing
through the kitchen window)
for my mother.

Choreography of Bounding

The game is we're sixteen.

I have pink & purple hair,
a pink & purple denim
backpack, & a boyfriend.

My sister tries to copy,
remoulding to match,
so I give her blue

hair & a green & blue
backpack—*sparkly blue*
I add & she beams

from under the trampoline.
We'll wear lipstick
I whisper, my mouth

hot against the grid
of black nylon
crosshatching her

cheeks with shadow,
poplar seeds floating
from our fingers,

summer snow in the grass.

After supper, dusk

tendrils wriggling from
the woods, I tell my sister
mid-leap

I can't play anymore.
To her shrinking
& slumping, her face

waning right
in front of me,
I lay out evidence:

upcoming grade seven
demands, the palpable
farce of pretend,

the choreography
of our bounding
too obvious,

& none of it real.

We'll be told to make up

but the second
I slip silver springs,
press feet

to night grass,
I've plucked worlds
from their orbits,

put them away like
marbles, my sister's eyes
bouncing off

my back, her hips
sunk & straining,
knees still bunched

before flight.

Straddled

In the basement of my friend's house, above a row of sharp silver saws & an open drawer of drill bits, hung these pictures pinned right to drywall, these girls in bright bikinis leaning over bikes, & I remember them as Pam Anderson, even Marilyn, but they were probably nameless. They straddled everything. I'd try to get a close look, soft wood shavings curling between my toes, & practice: the way they hooked hands to hips, their slack mouths. Nothing I had came close but one time my friend put her hand on my stomach & said I could totally pull off a belly button ring, so when I went home I chopped my T-shirt in half, lay flat on my bed, & slipped an earring to the fingertip-sized dip, bearing the weight of the metal to the centre of my being, & desperately wanting to dig it even deeper.

The Sacredness of Sleepovers

How I could never keep vigil,
needed waking to choose which teacher
to kill, marry, or screw, elementary
school songs like swears, like spells
shaking the walls of the spare room,
then sneaking our mothers' vodka,
the first time we sorted puzzle pieces
for hours before crumpling to confess
the ways we felt ourselves, the spaces
we'd found that made us ashamed.

How I once threw a whole cake on the floor
at the end of an all-nighter & we
scrubbed & scrubbed but the stain
on the unfinished wood still spread,
so, standing our ground, we filled
our mouths with ancient magics, spoke
our scriptures in candy-fuzz tongues.

How I wanted to loosen the knot
at the nape of your neck, escaped
from my attempt at a French braid,
you looking to me blurry & tangled,
telling me that he touched you
when you were just a kid.

How we pressed shirt sleeves to chins,
how our eyes burned that dark room,
& how the prayer that curled from our growing
lungs lengthened like smoke, stretching
up & up to safer sleep.

Age Apocalypse

When I was sixteen, this boy wanted me
to climb a silo on his farm, swing up

metal rungs so we could see our whole town
down there below, but I never did,

& never climbed the feedmill either—
these my prairie strongholds,

these skylines I thought would stay.
I climbed, instead, the bell tower

of that church in Piney, my friends & I
scrambling the decaying

steps stretched to steeple
so we could see the fire we'd followed,

its hum of smoke haunting some
farmer's field or old forest, I don't know,

& it was too far to touch us anyway,
this slow-moving splinter, its brief

opening, & us laughing
the way you do

when it's always been
the end of the world.

Each September We Went to See the Geese

& this was before condos built up
all around my hometown, back when
the neighbour boy had a secret. He said
I'll tell you when the birds land
because like magic they know
to fly & fall together, feather
the sky & call hollow
into a dusk dying to frost.

This was when I believed in secrets,
in that last hunching in cool grass
before pushing on slightly from summer,
when anything might happen, so small beneath
pressing bodies full of air

come suddenly down
onto the lake.

In Dusk

Tucked into my Oma's afghan,
his left big toe, painted pink,
pushes through. He snatches
a ladybug from the frayed
lawn chair's aluminum legs,
cottony with web.

You're lucky

he says to the inside
of his elbow while I
husk corn, drift spun gold
off the porch, & slide fingers
down exposed kernels,
each pocket full. Puncture
one with my thumb.

The delicate way he paws
his eyes, pokes the irises,
I feel lucky, practiced, aim
the green sheath out
over the lawn where it
disappears to dirt.

All the things you want
you'll eventually have.

Dunk the ear in the pot,
grab at his wriggling
toe, laugh. Later, he'll borrow
lipstick, lean towards the dingy
medicine cabinet, reach,
& wipe the glass clear.

Silos

That summer,
we wore too much
black & sat
on the heaters
in the hall,
stood in fields
with boys
named Jake
& Brett & Cole,
invited them
to our parties.

We lay on
trampolines
sucking ice
pops, plastic
wrappers
sticky across
our cheeks,
ran up piles
of gravel with
Slurpee straws in
our mouths,
slid all the way
down in dust.
The small
stones rubbed
our hands soft.

At summer's
end, I put
my arms in
your coat
& felt us turn
to memory:

how we screamed
into silos over
& over—
our own echo
startling, old,
tender as stars;

how I wrote lyrics
on your jeans,
pressed in thumb-
ink heartbeats;

how you rubbed holes
in the knees.

Of Earth Crumbling

we run barefoot
          bramble-hooked
                    & howling
          throw
paintballs at fence
          posts   pock
          marks
                    a mile
          out:
                      corn
                    stalks sun
  flower
faces
                        & green
                      wheat
                                        fists
              of   earth
  crumb ling
                                          the   whole
                                            root
                                  to   chew
    &
                      the   world
                                fan   ning
                              un
  der
us
                            as you
            ex   plain
                                  kisses

tracing
fur
rows
but I   know
it's   got
to be
bet   ter
than
this

a worm
soft
glim mer   ing
a long

my calf

I Promised No More Poems About the Moon

but look at you under it, & without
a jacket, & me sharing your gloves

so when we try the monkey bars, we lurch
one-handed, the metal too biting

for bare skin. I sing "Silent Night" in German
to make you laugh, except you don't—

you've got your face tilted to catch snow
on the soft centre of your lips, dimples

of our footprints in the field, & everything
you say falling out in fog, proof of you

hanging above our heads & the faded moon proof
of something too.

Wuthering:

A Comprehensive Guide

Early February & He Built Her a Nest

for Nigel,
who lived & loved & died
among a colony of concrete

Did you hear about the gannet
who fell in love with a stone bird
on an island off New Zealand?

He dove thirty metres into sea,
wide wings tipped black
& forward, each a full two metres

from his cooing body, all for her
flaked paint, preying spun waves,
clutching spasmed scales to surface.

He shaped her beds of seaweed,
twigs, & dirt, plied her for that
one blue egg—the only ache

of his infant heart, its shell
lullaby—& her throat,
promisingly aloft.

Eighty yellow heads reaching
for the reckoning, slender
& sky-billed as if seeking

his fast-beating hopes,
embedded rituals, clipped
desire.

Gannets, did you know, remain
together several seasons, & in
the wild, mates will look up

so close, the long
points of their beaks tap
the gentle urgency of flight.

I'm warned against
anthropomorphizing, but
you see it too,

right—his stretch to meet her
decoyed feathering,
sun-faded but real?

Cats, Definitely

In the glow of my touch-
screen he sends results
from the allergy test, bumps
up & down his forearm: horses, grass,
cats, definitely. I text *sailors at sea*
kept cats to ward away evil, ensure
a safe return & one night in spring
he coaxes me onto the handlebars
of his bicycle, where I taste salt,
pollen, see myself for a second
as the figurehead,
weeping. I'm certain he'll spill me
into the street but he laughs because
nothing that bad has ever happened
to you & when he leaves, he lint rolls
his shirt sleeves, collects the party
balloons I blew, abandons
the welcome home
banner. I wish him nausea
when cycling & my bike breaks
the next week. I find balloon shards
under the couch where my cat
hid them, our remains colourful
if deflated. My cat takes care of me,
knocks the top of her head
into my wrists while I'm reading,
bites my naked feet to swell
the skin, & I like this idea
of welts, spells, of somehow saving
my starboard side.

A Scary Time for Men

Do I sound
like all my aunties
lined up in a row?

My dad today
over a burger said
Why are men so terrible?

& I shook
my head heavy.
I'm watching

each Hitchcock
movie & like
Rear Window best, but

if I'm honest,
don't like any
of them much,

only the women,
their eyes knowing
how it goes,

how Hitchcock
obsessed & stalked
on set, liked his girls

proper
& pretty &
properly dead.

The script called
for these
genuine reactions,

one
true
scream—

his high-angle,
her open mouth,
our long sound.

Found Offering

My arms where they fall
rise with rash, angry
against the pillow.
To be true,
this has been my body's
reaction to everything,
unless I can leave it. A trick I do
know, fainting in church
again this spring. My mom
touched two cold fingers
to my lips. Remember Berlin?
I thought a lot about growing
those days, the tenderness
that goes into making
a person, lying down in St.
Johannes-Evangelist-Kirche
listening to a sound
installation. My artist friend
afterwards said the bad
things she's done left her
with boring words.
I loved her like that,
licking the foam
from the edge of her cup,
claiming ghosts.
& I'm not so scared
of haunting now, it seems
a comfort, my throat
squeezed sore
around this morning,

so I call angels out-reaching,
their long fingers scorched
against my temple. Last night
I woke just after three,
thinking a man was standing
above me shining
a flashlight. I couldn't
move, kept saying
I don't understand. I try again,
say it aloud to the dark stain
high on my white wall,
some trace of an old tenant.
I say it in Latin, Low
German, my body
a house to fail,
pray in. I met
a beautiful Belgian boy
in Berlin. He had strawberry
blond hair & dimples,
said *cacophony*,
won a beer-tasting
competition, & later
on the steps to that altar
I fell asleep. I dreamt I became
famous for a poem called
"Peace on Earth
etc." I dreamt my skin
slipped open, its needing
easy, the in-
breaking divine.

Ocean Organ

in which an imagined underwater organ turns corporeal

An exposition

You'd read descent
was the closest thing
to grace & you'd try
anything once,
twice,

it's not like you said
you were looking to get
reborn, just suggested
this was for your health

when asked,
which you were,
many times.

A development

Step barefoot to dock,
flippers stiff under one arm.
A crowd of concert-divers,
most paired, middle-aged, bulge
sticky wetsuits. One woman wears
a leather jacket, flips it flat, slides
keys to its pocket. You pat
yourself down, consider
what you too should leave
on shore.

Floating from the harbour
you shiver, scuba-ed.
Barges bellow, too far
to see. You feed a gull
a fry & it's ungrateful
while four men sing shanties
from the railing. Catch
the bassist's eye as he
wipes sea spray from his chin.
You know already, it'll be
an unsteady somersault
below the waves.

Maybe you'd hoped for
the feeling of your pastor's palm
on the crown of your head,
water lukewarmed from
a shallow clay bowl rivering
your neck but instead, slipped
open-mouthed into Atlantic,
your chest resists
tubed oxygen.

Grasp, mechanical,
for light.

Beside you, someone sweeps
her arms like wings,
almost applause above
the organist—small,
you think, smaller than she
should be. Her fingers
curl like melting ice.

She bends on her bench, begins,
& you miss the silence of hall,
raised baton, even that one stray
cough's ricochet, didn't expect
terror churning
breath through pipes,
bloomed then swallowed,
kelp seeking silver spires,
toying in the blue.

There is no disappearing,
only opening
clean, enormous,
the water too full,
fish low, startled,
specks of silt & limbs
treading, an angel choir
left in the flood.

Kick soft. This current
knows to erode,
string its audience,
shells along sand. Chord
& chord. Imagine
whale song, bodies
chasmed & calling,
shadowed out
in the deep.

Think to cry
back a chorus,
something welling
at the back
of your throat.

A recapitulation

Later you'll shrug, say it
sounded like shipwreck,
but you'll hum
the tremor, intoned
repercussions,
because of course

it's impossible
to dive into a cold body
without breaching
changed.

It's impossible
to hear much of
anything above
the moan of metal
pipe,

except, sometimes,
the blue of skin
unclasped
by God.

A Boat Is Not the Whole World

My cousin's face when she turns
reveals the shell of sun.
We reckon pulls, brace hips,
harmony to her brother
in the kayak just farther on.
He's chased an eagle the island over

while our canoe drags, caught
in the channel's throat.
Last night from the bottom
bunk she held a speaker,
slow music, to her ear. I could not
see her mouth, just the darkness
under it. My cousin tells me

Logs left too long will saturate & sink.
I imagine them under chalky waves,
red still with morning, hope
their skeletons grow sea legs.
You're not my type I tell the loon
by my blade, her trill seamless.
No foundling heart, she arcs

her neck, cranes
from our boat, her body some broad &
important trick. Envious, I slip
water around me like a dress while
my cousin draws her oar up across her knees.
How low she swings her palm.
When he left her,

I put a wet washcloth on her forehead,
fed her milk chocolate from a china plate.
Her index finger pulls ripples round, drowned
to the stems of our ancestor glacier—
if not run off, dried up, anyway, cringed
into this cottaged lake, its sponged shores.
We'll have fireworks tonight,

go out in the motorboat
wrapped in quilts & felt, sit reverent
for the bombastic tribute to air,
our wanting so unroofed, & the loon
will sound a whale nocturne in the mist.

When Cohen Dies

i.

My ex calls & I think twice
then answer from
under the covers
of my parents'
spare room, let him
recall last August
when I'd cut my foot
open on a stone
barely submerged
in the lake & liked
too much his fingers
curling my white gauze,
dripping salt water
where it stung,
him securing me
a wheelchair
at the art gallery,
the roof of his arms
leaning me through
those carpeted rooms,
walls of heads
in raincoats, colour
like plastic,
hard blue.

He wished he had more
art in his home,
would talk that way,

rubbing thumbs over
antique writing desks,
& later taking me down
to the river
where we caught
bullheads & though
I hobbled the bank
to hurl each back,
the big one he kept,
hooked its gills,
knuckled whiskers,
sliced open & spilled
guts gulping between
his palms like prayer
debrided on the beach.

He doesn't believe
in baptism he said,
elbows on each
side of me, & I do—

I do still
wait for water
eyes shut in the spare
room against
the soft, old sheet,
now November
& my ex sounds like
he got better.

ii.

A benediction:
that day along
muddy Assiniboine
a wasp drowned
in my beer
bottle's throat,
& wet I let
it sour my tongue—

Lord, he asked
for proof
of grace &
I was ready,
Leonard, but
embarrassed,
sloughed off
the body
in my spit
where it
squirmed
& flicked
little legs,
tried to lift
wings booze-
soaked 'til I
coffined it
in my hand,

wanting as
I've always
wanted—

to be
ministered to,
excused &
blessed, but

there, there,
written
in blood—

a song sure
in coming,
a call & answer
unending
endingending,
his voice
on the phone.

Os Justi

The mouth of the righteous speaketh wisdom,
and his tongue talketh of judgment.
The law of his God is in his heart;
none of his steps shall slide.
Psalm 37:30-31 (KJV)

Snow not yet cleared
after the latest crow's
storm, slush frozen up
stone steps, we walk
into the dark
mouth of the righteous.

Metal Os of organ
pipes mid-
breath, I hold
your hand while all
around the choir
alleluias psalms.
Church creaks,
speaketh wisdom
in Latin lifting the
rafters of our ribs
& his tongue

Do you recognize him
right in front of us?

talketh of judgment.

I thought it was him in the dark but wasn't sure.
Now I'm sure.

Your face frozen
& him—

In the floral shirt.

He smiles
in the cross-
light, friends
on either side of him,
the law of his God
is in his heart,
his eyes
closing in the
eight-part
amen.

I watch you keep
your eyes open
& at the refrain,
we flee,
a sweeping descant
echoing alleluia,
& none,
alleluia,
of his steps,
alleluia,
shall slide.

Wuthering: A Comprehensive Guide

I felt as if the sky was torn off my life.
—Anne Carson

i.

You found the body on the moor,
a windswept, broken thing. You found
the body mid-dive, trying for lake,
you somehow knowing the body
likes promises earthy, stretched
along straight lines of dirt
where its greenness might
turn good.

The body lets you think you found it yourself.

ii.

The body believes
it could watch you talk
about roots, prairie grass, seed security
all day & in that way the body
does not think love is
an impossibility. The body burns
red in triangles, maps
circles from your collarbone
to your chest, pokes breath to
your inner ear,
seeks sun, craves water
& also you.

The body unfurls.

iii.

The whole city is coming
apart, but quiet. The body is interested
in quietness. At the bar, a band
plays so the body
leans into you & likes the feeling,
flannel at its neck.
The body slowly bends,
puts its beer between
your feet & you
guard it, a blackbird
with its egg. Later in your car
parked up the scarp,
the body looks to see sky
a sheet dissolving,
yellow, black, electric,

the body's hush.

iv.

The body swells an idea:
moving west,
growing in the rain,
building real muscle.
At the same time,
the body is filling
its apartment with
plants & pets & becoming
attracted to ways
of generating home
knowledge. You tell
the body you are trying
to see the tree so that
you might describe it.

> The body says *In my dream I am out on the moor*
> *& you are smashing your forehead against the*
> *bark of an ash.*

v.

You went north instead
of coming back to the body so the body
creeps out to the moon
to commune. The body
does not want to tell
anyone about your
deep distance, the way you
ask, or don't, while it falls
out of itself, how the world
drops serious & fierce,
bizarrely bright,
from the sky.

The body rotates a galaxy.

vi.

Sodden, satisfied, you
return, take the body,
push its palms up under
your shirt. You say *I am*
now safe but the body narrows
against the window,
folds over the kitchen
sink rubbing small
ceramic cups, old church
mugs after midnight,
the curtains worn blue
& floating, back
& forth like whispers.

The body squints; a ghost cycles in the garden.

vii.

The body becomes
direct about its desires. *Your fingers*
the body says *dipping into & out*
of the lake. Your sun-hot neck
touched gently. The huge
& heavy silence, the inevitable
sinking, the strange bird, the water
stirring then stilled

up on the rocks. & the body.

viii.

You bring morning
coffee, cross the street with
white paper cups, your apology, an omen.
From the balcony, the body rattles
the rusted metal railing,
anticipates the air
change, smells thunder.

& then the body battens down.

ix.

In the field, pink clover, golden
aster, purple dropseed, harebell.
The wind here hurtles to horizon
so the body lies low, the soil
& the body outstretched,
forsaken,
absolved.

The body slips free a blade, nibbles the long root.

x.

Finally, the body feels
its way to a house
out of the wind. There
the body learns to dance whole
routines, cook soups & stews,
sleep soundly. The body
recalls the moor & thinks of you fondly
or not at all; the body has set
certain blocks & other bodies
no longer scare it. People laugh
when the body begins
to read & tell stories.

They sit at the body's feet, which, each night,
trace soil up the stairs.

You Could Blow Up the Whole World & End Up Feeling Sorry for Yourself

I've been obsessing over Marilyn Monroe & I think I might be in love with her—me & everyone else. I've been having stress dreams about my ex-lovers. They keep sitting next to me wearing too many hats. Sometimes we're in a church, sometimes we're in a park, sometimes we're in a bar. *It's me, don't you remember? The tomato from upstairs.* I am trying to memorize one good Marilyn monologue, but I just can't do the voice. Sometimes I fantasize about my ex-lovers dying. It is because they seem happy & I seem unhappy but it's not that I want them to be dead so much as I want them to be sad & bald. After Marilyn died, Arthur Miller said he wouldn't go to her funeral because *she won't be there* & that made me weep walking down Portage drinking McDonald's coffee. I don't have murder in me, probably. I'm learning to sit still with what is in me & forgive myself for it. *How do you find your way back in the dark?* Just yesterday I shared a beer with one ex-lover while he told me he was sorry & also that he is trying to think of a reason for doing everything that he is doing, which I couldn't relate to. I'm trying to be less dramatic, but I also want everyone to pay attention to me as though I am having a crisis, which I am not, *so you pull yourself together, you go on to the next job, the next saxophone player*. The newest experiment of my life is that I'm trying to only wash my hair once a week & the cycle of grease & self-denial has been extremely affirming. While I take my baths & do not wash my hair, I practice monologues for the two cats watching from the mat. *A stairway to nowhere! I think that's just elegant* & I don't hate Arthur Miller at all, which I realize makes me part of the problem. I used to think I would be the sort of person who would attract love very easily but I'm coming to grips with the fact that there aren't really reasons for very many things, though maybe *that's what I'm running away from* when, sitting beside my ex, our knees touch, just once, under the table.

I can tell you one thing: it's not going to happen to me again. Ever.

At Least Light

Halcyon's axial tilt
up the frozen river takes her
to birds nested beneath famine
months lifting throats to
frostbite moon, stretch sun
unconquered, pale.

To the birds, she cries
Soon; after all, the year will be
reborn & she has finished
calling for her morning
star, who sank quickly,
just a stone.

Hibernal solstice heats
to fog, so she traces the earth
standing still &
she & him—opposite
points in the sky.

She loved too long but now
these seven days without
storm, set on each side of
winter's summit, open
like a bed, celestial.

Gods turned them both to birds,
in the past. Her feeling is
the world is mostly sky;
the year might still reverse.

Powerful Millennials on the California Freeway

Vermiculture

i.

Kim's roommate worm-composts,
sells bins of wriggling redemption,
& in their basement I kneel
next to the litter box by the water
heater & watch worms slip
through earth, fleshy
& gobbling blind.

> Give us your eggshells,
> your apple cores, gorge
> us on regret. See how we till it all over,
> munch invisible mouths. Track
> the tiny gnathic movements
> digesting disaster.

ii.

As a child, I learned to bisect worms
on the sidewalk, loose new life with
each swift slice. *Got more*
than one brain in there I was told.
It'll grow what's missing. Now I know
the worm may survive the split,
but only the head half, & anyway,
these surgeries weren't meant to be cruel,
transfixed as I was by the survivability
of everything: ants emerging from baseboards,
crocuses after frost, a cluster
of fungi in the ditch grass.

iii.

When fishing with Kim up in Gimli,
she curled my hook right through
a worm, a weave of pink spun to barb.
I looked away from the softened snag
luring below grey water, feared
the awful interruption of my line.
We threw the fish all back, born-again,
but even the moon is due for disintegration,
orbital decay gnawing the space between us.

> Well, pull in, come on closer.
> Tap the glass. Trace
> our squirming efforts at reform.
> Watch how we bury what's dead.

Something Good

Laura, meanwhile, says

Why is it so easy to die alone?

& I tell her I'm doing yoga now, lying on the rug I got from Morocco, phone screen-down & pulsing. The skeletal camels stitched under me rise up, a sign, but I tell Laura we're doing fine. I don't think she believes me.

We're going to die in our beds with our heaters cranked up all the way. Don't you see it?

See what? I say & her dogs are barking. Okay, yes, my hair is falling out, I whisper. It's everywhere, on my floor & woven into my fleece pajamas, in my socks, on my sheets, & I think I need to drink more water. Laura says

This apocalypse is made of Triscuits & peanuts & dried apricots.

Snow cracks white against the window's dark mouth. I say we go out with something good, something like the night we went down to the beach during the blizzard.

Remember the frozen sand, how we laughed, watched the world float off in fog?

Laura says. She says

Do you remember?

& then she's quiet so I close my eyes. One last computer screen glows & this is how they find us: curled up bones on old brown rugs, page-a-day calendars, half-knitted scarves, the lampshades we painted, feathers unglued & drifting.

> *Pen on Post-its, that sad North African proverb*
> *you like—*

only the words we really mean.

Orbit

After the funeral,
we took off
our shirts & sat
backyard in our bras,
thought to water
the tomatoes
but instead drank
radlers, diagnosed
each other
astrologically, fell
asleep with red
shoulders, shocked
the world could
still reach us,
shocked our skin
still held sun.

This Bridge Symbolizes Hope

You're almost there Julia says through the phone but she
doesn't know where I am, how far from home, how
the river crushes black ice below. That's just how she is,
promising easy even in winter, painting yellow

flowers & saucers on the raw cotton of her dress,
pulling crystal crumbs from her pockets, a husk
of geode for us to smash. Hoists a hammer & trusts
in the reveal of real glitter forged by earth's soft tremors

in the under-crust. When her strike ricochets
& the rock rolls coffee table to carpet uncracked, she taps
the hammer's head against her knee, explains *everything*
opens eventually & I think about the night she caught

on fire at a Gastown bar but still got some guy's number,
how we slept in the nest of our apartment:
a futon piled with blankets, pillows, our Nintendo 64. How
in the morning, I shook singed hair from Julia's head,

held ash in a heap on my fingertip, & she closed her eyes
to blow her DNA out around us like snow, like
we were always meant to lose these small parts, like
we only had to wait for something better.

You still there? Julia asks. I slip my way to sidewalk
& tell her *yes* & she says *good* & I believe her.

Molly Learns Her Astrology

Okay, tell me again
about water, her sun
in cardinal Cancer,
her Pisces rising.
Makes sense, her
nightly baths,
secrets liquid
in her belly.

One night she
stumbles the spring
snow under a streetlamp,
examines the wet slice
of moon, radical
rearrangement
of her life,

the pink of ice,
frozen slopes
of mud. She says
I hold too many
too willingly
then fills,

she says *I fill*
the shape of my container.

Communion

We turn to ritual, dyeing each other's hair in the bathrooms of the houses we housesit. We stain the counters, paint bruising the laminate. We do not make everything into a metaphor, try knitting. Accumulating mildew & fruit flies, we drink from mason jars left under a full snow moon, push bare hands into grey slush & wash the car with it. A coyote running along the river stops to stare. How embarrassing, our howls, our tilting to sky. We splash the pin-ups by the bathtub, collages we clipped from old Playboys, & replace them, cut careful halos around their heads. We perform at parties & nail the lifts. Often, we open our eyes at night to see someone kneeling by the nightstand or curled in the closet. They are crouched & confessing. They are denying. They are grinning with small, sharp teeth. Upon waking, we conjure probiotics, brew & ferment. We search the carpet for claws the cat has shed, place them points up under our pillows. We find a little dead bird on the windowsill, bury it in the tomato plant. We sit around on the kitchen floor. A box of red wine & the mugs our mothers made. We tell each other some of what has happened to us. Something has happened to all of us, our telling teaching us this. It helps to say it happened, to do this in remembrance. It helps to say: this body, this blood. To say: me too, me too.

Burrowing

The polar bear head at FortWhyte Alive
considers the dust that coats her plastic tongue—
she craves bite, dreams blood, hears a burrowing
owl, sprinter, long-legged in the late afternoon.
In chase, the bear's frozen jaw confesses:

i would gather for you

crickets, ground beetles, young mourning doves.
The owl enclosure beams earthy sanctuary, damp wood
cleaved open.

i don't sleep either

no hibernation unhaunted. A woman daily counts prairie
dog & bird bodies, watches for breath below ground.
Then, cheek hot on freshwater aquarium,
she asks murky muscle, old eyes, how to be less
human. The burrowing owl, a juvenile, tucks down
into dirt, hopes vaguely but deeply for diverted
tunnels, while bear huffs to the lady wishing fish,
their skitter, stone-flash:

i miss arctic

char, seal, inukshuk hailing shale, spray paint like moss

i miss

soil turning, a world even broke up &
melted, ghosts darting tall grass,
flocking for home.

Broken Seals All Summer

By glass, I'm impossibly close,
try to read something in the glazed
female face, seven gorillas in all; a sign
says *Survival Breeding Plan.*
The crowd looks & laughs.
                        Seven a reference
                                to creation recite my friends
                                returned with read palms—
                                they'll live at least to seventy
                                so long as they get real
                                on health. I am interested in healing,
                                but the world's beyond it,
                                the spectacular rotation, found even
                                in the spirals
                        of our thumbs.
We scroll images of orca
heaving her baby's corpse above waves,
seventeen days a wake: take us,
take up us.
                        How to honour this looming
                                knowing? Offer evocation
                                of wholeness: *seven.* Dance ocean
                                proverb to dust, spit, bacteria
                                growing legs to stand on, the shifting
                                DNAs extravagant
                        in despair.
From our porch, worms
drip sticky thread. The canopy
infested, elms stretched white
& ragged, I see a circus,

squirming satellites, a womb
collecting membranes
delicate with dignity, purled
to tightly knitted bones.
                We text our doom
                        free-bleeding, save seeds,
                        crystal-clutch. Of course,
                        preserves won't keep
                        horizon from shrapnel
                in the haze:

        light & dark,

water
from water,

        the gathering
        of earth,

                seasons,

        & stars,

                        then moving
                        creatures
                        & beasts

—our image: I hear it coming.

I, Too, Am the Mountaintop

i.

Laura smashed both ankles
falling from a rock in Joshua Tree,
looked up to find everything
at wrong angles.

The boyfriend
moved to LA but
she kept the dogs.

The boyfriend
moved to LA so
she moved eerie,
inward to the desert.

When I went to see her,
we watched holes along the path
suspicious of snakes

& I became very biblical,
told Laura about Joshua
& heathen Jericho,

her helpful whores,
the one red cord,
trumpets calling down
each sandy column
of the world.

ii.

After the fall, the dogs
flopped out in sun while
Laura on painkillers
sent fried egg emojis again &
again: *forty days & all that.*

For now that she's scrambled
like some scorpion thing
through sand, she lets me

kiss the breaks
in her prophecy, tuck bones
into old potato sacks

full of camel hair,
honey, wilderness
proclaiming a new
pilgrimage

& us beloved,
hosanna, under
all this falling sky.

Eclipse from Mont-Royal

Peaches filling our cheeks, we dare
not squint the sun but stick legs deep
into grass, watch clouds belly-up.
So maybe we go home Karla says

maybe that would be better for our health.
We talk about our health now,
at least, & the belugas who died
in Vancouver calling for Arctic,

round heads ballooning song.
The next day when it pours,
we'll run roads turned river.
It will rain like it does in Vancouver,

or like it does everywhere.
On the bus, when a stranger
slaps Karla because she is pretty,
drenched, but not his, she'll say

pardon & we will get off at
the next stop. His fingers will
sting the skin red around her
closed mouth & I'll tell her *I'm sorry*

but today, our cheeks sweeten
with peach, moon swings into sun,
& we talk as though the light,
when it flips out from shadow,
          will be on our side.

Vitreous

Jill pulls from her velvet
drawstring two crystals,

balances them in the soft-
peddled auditorium:

synthetic down coats
stuffed under red

chairs, a cello, stand-up bass,
grand old piano, the intention

of heart. Yesterday
we bolted four lanes

of traffic, squeaked snow
with our boots while she

screamed *Atria, vena*
cava, valves, ventricles!

Blood I said & spat
right onto the ground.

Last week, Jill ran her toenails
clean off. Now, she slips

clear quartz to the left breast
pocket of her denim jacket;

an amethyst she pops in
her mouth, the world

sudden, swallowed, sure,
but we've the four pure chambers

of this blue-moon month &
we are healing, purple-tongued.

Resurrection Except as Metaphor

In my spaceship dream
I tell my sister-in-law
we became old-timey detectives.
She yawns, her son wailing down
the beach. *A murderer was loose,*
but we trapped him in a faulty escape pod
& I stretch my eyes to show
how I am remembering.

She told me once, after a bad breakup,
that I could do whatever I wanted:
go to his house, scream through
the window, pee in his garden, but I
couldn't stand to be so grounded,
preferred instead a kind of weightless
guessing, zero gravity over asteroids,
a focus on other fast-burning stars.

Those days, to fall asleep, I read
Thus Spake Zarathustra, a copy
from my brother, his way to say
it's okay to distrust all resurrection
except as metaphor. That same Christmas,
my brother, fully-grown,
got a remote-control plane
& we crashed it again & again
in the basement before
we lost it to the woods.

My sister-in-law opens her phone
to a fine-dusted Curiosity rover.
It took a space selfie she says & I squint
at its broad shell, imagine Mars,
hard, open claws, a faulty escape.

Someone flies a drone flat & low,
skimming sand then whirring up
to a speck spoiling clouds.
My brother swoops his son to shoulder
where he shouts, toddler-pitch:
Goodnight tiny airplane! hands
flung up, wide open, waving.

Astronomical

Rosa Barba's exhibition *Send Me Sky, Henrietta*
flutters the cosmos on ribbons of film, photographic
plates projecting galaxy glow to canvas. See,
Henrietta S. Leavitt learned to measure the universe,
discovered variable stars & catalogued
their brightness from the basement of Harvard.
My friend Rebecca reaches her hand
to the beam of light, body becoming first a
flicker, then an asteroid, a black hole.
We seek deep space, wrapped in the sediment
of earth, its sickly spin. Remember, Rebecca's painting
pulled from a show at the VPL due to complaints
of nudity, the woman's thick thighs, her smirk,
her clenched fist lifting her pale yellow skirt.
Rebecca examined her plastic strings swinging from
chains holding nothing
—what would it have been like to see them take her down?—
then spread a tarp in the parking lot
ripped paper from the roll in her trunk, shook
& sprayed pink&yellow&green&black galactic, wrote
we will come back! stood on a table to suspend it
in her painting's empty space. Luminous. Send us
this sky, Henrietta, send us spectral shifts, slipping
strata, lifted skirts, send us your standard candle
to light up the whole impossible expanse,
light up, light up, light up, & measure us
immense.

Powerful Millennials on the California Freeway

got lost pointing to huge white wind
turbines & outlet malls

Laura missing him said she'd
love a song like Springsteen

so when the radio started *Dancing*
in the Dark we screamed

slammed the horn &
careened through strange

desert sand ridiculous brushy palms
rolled down the borrowed-car top

something happening
somewhere! what else

might we invoke
waving iced coffees

to the sun

Grainy to Froth; Red to Burst

I cried on
the phone
to Wendy
as I walked
down Wolseley,
eighteen gardening
hippie dads
averting their
eyes. One of
those first hot
spring days
with worms
noodling the
sidewalk, bird
crescendos lifting
the petalled
planet green
& wet from
winter's womb
& me, wanting
to die. Wendy
remembered the
time we took
the bus to Seattle
in February, stood
in the wind
at the pier, our
necks twisted
up to see all

that grey ocean
heaving itself
into concrete,
collapsing
grainy to froth.
The curdled
earth she cooed
returns with
an onslaught
of rot. I was
staring at a
particular
tulip bathing
above the mulch
in sweetest ten
a.m. sun, beaming
red to burst.
Gasped into
the phone,
unzipped my
fleece, *Wendy*
I said, ducking
my head, flower
blurred between
blinks, *I am*
going to eat up.
Brushed my
nose against
small seeds,

rouged my
cheek, kissed
then tore
pollen tender
between the
rubber of gums
giggling pigment:
yes, that's what
I'll do, I'll eat
this whole
world up.

Notes on the Poems

"Early February & He Built Her a Nest"

In February 2018, a New Zealand gannet nicknamed Nigel No-Mates was found dead on Mana Island surrounded by over eighty concrete birds. Conservation officers created the replicas in an attempt to attract gannets & repopulate the island, but Nigel, arriving in 2013, was the first & only (real) bird to make Mana his home. Nigel fell in love with one decoy in particular &, for the last five years of his life, groomed her feathers, brought her fish, & built her nests. He died beside her.

"Ocean Organ"

Commissioned by Earth World Collaborative, this poem was inspired by André Forget's short story "The Lower Registers" which describes a musicologist's study of a fictional instrument, the Hydroörganon—an underwater organ.

"When Cohen Dies"

Karel Funk's hooded figure paintings exhibited at the Winnipeg Art Gallery in 2016 inspired the line "walls of heads in raincoats." The blue raincoats are also a reference to Leonard Cohen's famous jacket. The words "there, there / written in blood" come from Cohen's lyric "It's written there in blood" in "Ain't No Cure for Love."

"Os Justi"

"Os justi" ("The mouth of the righteous") is a Gregorian chant composed by Anton Bruckner. Its text comes from Psalm 37.

"Wuthering: A Comprehensive Guide"

This poem was written under the influence of *Wuthering Heights*. Its epigraph comes from Anne Carson's meditations on heartbreak & Emily Brontë in "The Glass Essay."

"You Could Blow Up the Whole World & End Up Feeling Sorry for Yourself"

A number of Marilyn Monroe quotes are used in this poem. The title & the line "How do you find your way back in the dark?" are from Monroe's character Roslyn in *The Misfits*. As "The Girl" in *The Seven Year Itch*, Monroe says, "It's me, don't you remember? The tomato from upstairs," &, "A stairway to nowhere! I think that's just elegant." In *Some Like it Hot*, Sugar, played by Monroe, says, in the same monologue: "So you pull yourself together. You go on to the next job, the next saxophone player," "That's what I'm running away from," &, "It's never going to happen to me again. Ever."

"At Least Light"

After Zeus shipwrecked Alcyone's beloved husband, Ceyx, Alcyone threw herself into the sea. Moved by her grief, the gods turned the couple into kingfishers, or halcyon birds. The seven days on each side of the winter solstice are known as Halcyon Days, a period of time when Alcyone's father, Aeolus, calms the winds so that Alcyone can lay her eggs on the beach in safety. These days signal a brief break in the storm.

"Broken Seals All Summer"

This poem relays the creation of the world as told in Genesis. The number seven symbolizes completion, as exemplified in Genesis 2:1-2 ("Thus the heavens and the earth were finished, and all the host of them. And on the seventh day God ended his work which he had made; and he rested on the seventh day from all his work which he had made.") & Revelation 5:1 ("And I saw in the right hand of him that sat on the throne a book written within and on the backside, sealed with seven seals.").

"Eclipse from Mont-Royal"

In November 2016, Aurora, the Vancouver Aquarium's last beluga whale, died. The total solar eclipse of August 2017 is the event observed in the poem.

"Resurrection Except as Metaphor"

In the fall of 2018, NASA released the "space selfie" captured by the Mars Curiosity rover. *Thus Spake Zarathustra* is a philosophical novel by Friedrich Nietzsche & also a tone poem by Richard Strauss, famous for its use in *2001: A Space Odyssey.*

"Astronomical"

In 2018, Saskatoon's Remai Modern art museum hosted Rosa Barba's exhibition *Send Me Sky, Henrietta.* The project is named after Henrietta S. Leavitt, an American astronomer who discovered that by calculating the luminosity of stars, she could measure intergalactic distances.

Acknowledgements

Some of these poems, or versions of them, have appeared in *SAD Mag, Arc Poetry Magazine, Dear Journal, Prairie Fire,* the *Winnipeg Free Press, Poetry Is Dead, Contemporary Verse 2,* & as part of an Earth World Collaborative project.

Thank you to Jamis, Sharon, & Melissa at Turnstone Press for making this book with me. Thank you to Sharon especially for your immense editorial insight, for finding a shape for all of these sounds.

Thank you to Jeanette Lynes & the MFA in Writing at the University of Saskatchewan for the financial support which enabled me to attend the 2019 Sage Hill Writing Experience poetry colloquium & learn from Sandra Ridley. Thank you, Sandra, for your generous attention & encouragement on this manuscript.

Thank you to Jennifer Still for showing me all the places I might look for poems & for seeing a book in what I brought to your desk.

Thank you to my poetry professors Rhea Tregebov & Sheri Benning, & to my high school English teacher Barry Dyck. Your classrooms are some of my favourite places.

Thank you to my mom & dad for your unconditional support & for teaching me to love words.

&, thank you to my dear friends & family whose strength & power inspired the writing of much of this book: Lynette, Lisa, & Karin; Gerald & Matthew; Karla, Jill, Jami, Erin S, Erin F, Molly, Rebecca, LL, Haley, & Rachel; Laura & Julia & Rebecca; Kim & Catherine; Wendy & Monika; Wes & Walker; Kathryn; Jeannine, Emily W, Emily M, Nicole, Jess, Beth, Jack, & Natalie. I am lucky to live in a world with such a bright & constant canopy of stars.